MW01223745

Each Month I Sing

by

L. Luis López

ISBN 978-0-9818339-1-0

Cover Graphic by Deborah Snider
Book & Cover Design: Linda Lane

Farolito Press
P.O. Box 60003
Grand Junction, Colorado 81506

For every teacher who has touched the minds

of others, we belong to the greatest profession imaginable.

This collection of poems is made up of twelve poems for each month.

The first poem for each month is about the name of the month, the second is inspired by its gem, the third by its flower, the fourth by the zodiac sign it enters under, the fifth by a famous writer born during the month, and the sixth by a famous painter born during the month. The remaining six are my own observations about and my experiences with the month. An additional poem introduces each month by listing the matter for the first six poems. The title, *Each Month I Sing*, is meant to be an echo of how the great epic poets like Homer, Virgil, and Milton called upon their muses for inspiration.

Each month has been my inspiration.

Table of Contents

January

for Janus
Roman god of doorways

Garnet its gem
Carnation the flower

enters
beneath
the goat-fish Capricorn

Carl Sandburg
and
Paul Cezanne
born
          this month

Midnight, January 1

Dim in the yellow of my lantern,
Janus,
I stand before your garden gate,

looking at you
looking behind me,

your face,
in the flicker of shadows, a blank.

I push open the gate,
Janus,
step within and shut it.

I look at you
looking before me,

your face,
in the flicker of shadows, a blank.

Were I a carver of faces,
Janus,
I would etch

the blank face looking behind
with
                lines of dismay.

I would etch

the blank face looking ahead
with
                lines of fright.

Janus, Roman God of two faces, featured on gates and doorways, one facing in,
one facing out.

Noah's Garnet

A giant garnet sways from a beam
in the lowest level
of the Ark,
its gentle glow
helps Noah tend the animals.

Beneath the glow he toils
in stench,
red his sweat,
God's chosen enduring
hours in the bowels of the deep.

Folklore: Some believe Noah hung a large garnet in the Ark for light. The garnet
is thought to have an inner light.

Ode to the Carnation

That ancient Greek botanist, Theophrastus,
named you *dianthus*,
divine flower,
and oh divine you are in your beauty,

even in your common name, carnation,
color of flesh from which
incarnation, God made flesh, derives.

I hear tell you are also called clove pink,
clove your fruit in shape of nail
resembling that
driven through the Savior's hand and feet.

But I remember you when I was seven,
divine another way—

your name and picture on a can of
condensed milk
sitting on the kitchen table,

my grandmother pouring your milk
into her morning coffee,
onto my cream of wheat,
over my raspberry jello at dinner's end.

Ah! The taste! You, oh, Theophrastus,
and you, oh Christ,
were you here
would agree,
divine the flower, and, oh, divine the taste
in coffee, jello, and cream of wheat.

Capricorn

Though your name means
hornéd goat,
you are half fish . . .

how
does your story go?

Frightened by the mighty
serpent, Typhon,
you
jump into the sea, hooves first,

hoping to become fish,

but
realizing the serpent
can swim,

change

your

mind

in midtransformation.

Typhon, a gigantic hundred-headed monster, created by Gaea to destroy the
Olympian gods.

With Apologies to Carl Sandburg

Pile them high in Iraq and Afghanistan,
Shovel them under and let me work—

I am the worm, I devour all.

I devour Iraqi, Afghani, Americani, and otheri.
So far four thousand and more Americani.
The U.S. Government won't tell me
How many Iraqi, Afghani, and otheri.

Pile them high in Iraq and Afghanistan.
Shovel them under and let me work—

I am the worm, I devour all.

Italicized words, phrases, and lines from Carl Sandburg's "Grass."

L. Luis López

Cézanne's *Card Players*

this time Cézanne
paints three men in hats
at a table,
each cupping a set of cards,
one hand holding,
the other ready to tap the
number needed—

stands back, looks at it,
then paints
another man in hat standing
behind
looking over the shoulder
of the man nearest
him,
and to the standing man's
left,
paints four pipes in a rack
on the wall—

it is then I notice the
white pipe
lying on the table,
stem inward,
open bowl facing the man
on the left—

turning to me,
Cézanne points his brush
at the canvas,

"if you
are wondering,
this painting of a table, hats,
hands,
and pipes is about
four hard lives forgetting."

resolana

> winter snow lying north
> of home
> receives
> no smile from warmth from sun
>
> not like the south
> where
> cat and dog
> curl
> in warmth of sun and wall

resolana: the sunny side of a home

five a.m.

within the street
lamp
cone of light

snowflakes cast
shadows

that scurry
along the sidewalk
to meet
their falling mates

there
snowflakes
become accumulation

shadows annihilation

fog

fog fills the space between
cottonwood branches
this
winter evening, her
cold swirls
lit
by the corner streetlamp

at dawn
she
lies frozen on the branches,
white crystals
awaiting
the morning blush

except for the shadow

seems larger than
it is this
pebble on the sidewalk

shadow cast
by two-thirty sun
reveals
the shape of its top

three jagged peaks

fact

I would not know
except
for the shadow

even the unseemly

the morning sun
halos

each cattail along the ditch,

a misty splendor
transforming unseemly fuzz,

as though the Pope

with
Sign of Cross

had
sainted each one

when I pass on

sometimes I think I'm about
to leave this world,
I note
such beauty on harshest days

today

brittle puffs on sagebrush branch
lift
in gold, oh gold, scatter

up, out, away

at touch of gentle hand,

when I pass on
would it would be in such a way

February

after *februa*
Latin for cleansing

Amethyst its gem
Violet the flower

receives
the pouring waters of Aquarius

Henry Wadsworth Longfellow
and
Norman Rockwell
born

          this month

Each Month I Sing

februa

februa, Roman feast
of purification,
defines
the month of February
whose
zodiac sign hovers
unseen
in the sky of day

are you unclean?

stretch
forth your arms,
cup
your hands,
catch
the purifying water
as
Aquarius pours

wash
eyes, nose, mouth,
and ears
of spent fiery passions

undress, let
the water run over
your body

yes, wash
in the waters of Aquarius

wash during *februa*
February
the month of purification

Amethyst for Preciliano

if we had known the amethyst
was your birthstone,
Preciliano,
that agéd liquid from the grape
would not have
fouled
you with lurid laughter,
filled
you with utter sadness,
turned
you to violent anger—

yet
you often touched it,
praised it in youthful days
for
you and I
made radios, listened
to the world,
thinking
the purple quartz a miracle
just
not knowing that crystal's
power over the fermented grape

Folklore: The amethyst was thought to have supernatural powers. It brought luck, ensured constancy, and protected against magic. It was worn as an amulet against drunkenness.

first love, second grade, Violet

second grade, first seat,
first row,
Violet
sits in front of me

lavender her dress,
her scent,
ribbon in her hair

Violet,
first love, sits in front of me

Violets are linked to love. Puck uses their juice in *A Midsummer Night's Dream*.
The violet is also associated with an innocent, unspoiled love.

A Sonnet for Aquarius

This month begins with the sun in your stars,
Aquarius. Rain from your pouring cups
Will fill our rivers, flood our plains in hopes
Of growth when the sun moves to Aries' house.
One time the pouring surged out of control.
Fomalhaut, the fish's mouth, could hold no more,
So rivers overflowed, no lake could store
The rush, the earth was soaked from pole to pole.
That time in anger Zeus helped drown the world
With shake of aegis black and thunder clash,
And lit, relit the pour with lightning flash
To make man feel and see that anger hurled.
God-guests be welcome in our homes next time,
Aquarius, so Zeus your cups keep calm.

Mythology: Because Zeus was badly treated as a guest in many homes, he pun-
ished mankind with a flood. Only Baucis and Philemon were saved since they
treated their unknown guests, Zeus and Hermes, with courtesy.

A Clerihew for Longfellow

Henry Wadsworth Longfellow
Translated the *Inferno* below
Into the English language
To teach us how we might languish.

A clerihew is a light verse invented by Edmund Clerihew Bentley. It is made up of two couplets rhyming aabb with a famous person named in the first rhyme. Others appear in this collection.

Traffic Conditions by Norman Rockwell

A little bulldog sits uncertain
before a huge
red alley-filling truck,
Pepies No 532
reads the sign on driver's side
door
and simply Pepies
on the cab, the cargo box,
and the other door.

The bulldog is unsure
of the attention
it is receiving from twenty
surrounding
pairs of eyes, arms
and hands extended,
coaxing
it to get out of the way.

The little dog in this painting
is more than the normal
obligatory dog
asleep under the table,
spread at its master's feet,
looking from behind
this or that,
running with children,
hunting with hunters,
or
resting its chin on its owner's lap.

No,
this dog is front and center,
truck bumper
one foot above its head,

looked on
by a lady cyclist,
a frightened lady hands to head,

a frowning man, pipe in mouth,
a baby with sagging diaper,
a violin teacher,
a violin student with haughty
mother,
a window washer,
an artist and his model,
the driver of the truck,
and others

including
a white dove, wings outspread,
like
the Holy Ghost
hovering above to the right.

So many eyes
Intent
on the bulldog,
sitting
uncertain before the huge
red alley-filling truck,
Pepies No 532,
its bumper
one foot above the little dog's head.

at the 7th street café

the lady in green   her husband in grey
blouse   wool shirt
and grey hat   and red baseball cap
sits   sits
heavy in the booth   slim across from her
choosing   stirring
sweet n' low   four sugars
n' skim   into his
over sugar bowl   please
n' cream   leave two fingers
for   for cream"
her steeping breakfast tea steaming coffee mug

puff white high desert blossoms

this a.m.
late February snow
forms
puff white blossoms
on
sagebrush tops

hundreds
no thousands of
single puffs
become solid white
in desert field
stretching
far
to that
flat top mountain

puff
blossoms
not visited
by butterfly or bee

by noon
each blossom
will melt drip by drop
onto the desert
floor
there
to
spur the growth

of true
sagebrush
blossoms by spring

these
visited
by butterfly and bee

Four A.M.

I watch a dark cloud,
in form of wolf,
swallow the moon,
jaws wide,
no struggle, just a glow
slipping
dim,
dimmer,
dark into its waiting belly.

Dark Skoll I fear!

And knowing the story,
I think to wait
for light of day,
wonder
if within the
thickening clouds,
Hati,
that other wolf,
has already swallowed the sun,
jaws wide,
no struggle,
just a glow having slipped
dim,
dimmer,
dark into its waiting belly.

I fear with halt in heart
there will be
no light of day and feel
now
I understand
the Norse concerning Ragnarok.

Mythology: According to the Norse, three wolves will be involved in Ragnarok, the end of the world, Skoll, Hati, and Fenrir.

I never noticed the thaw

I never noticed the thaw underfoot
at February's end,

being a somewhat city boy raised
in a part of town where streets
were paved
and sidewalks ran from house
to store to church to school
to barbershop
and all the way downtown, my
feet seldom
landing on sand, or dirt, or mud,

so I never noticed the thaw underfoot
at February's end.

Eye

sky is so beautiful

the   today

I

feel   God

I am in the I of

Flora
para mi abuela on her birth month

Four steps lift from the traffic infested
street
to your enclosed forest like
porch
where canaries and parakeets tweet in
cages,

haven from the world of wheel and horn,
place
to which a crying child can run, climb,
knock,
and fall into your welcoming comfortable
arms,

gramma, your aroma, the cooking of
beans,
chile, and tortillas, your soft voice among
the chirp
of birds soothing a child's frustrations.
Flora

I hope you can see I have built a forest
porch,
where canaries and parakeets tweet in
cages,
fours steps lifting from the traffic infested
street,

to which a crying child may run, climb, knock,
and fall
into my own welcoming comfortable arms.

Each Month I Sing

March

named for Mars
Roman god of war

Aquamarine its gem
Daffodil the flower

below
the two fish of Pisces

Robert Frost
and
Vincent Van Gogh
born
            this month

As you approach April

March, like Mars, your
namesake,
you leave February

dressed in battle gear, enter
on military feet,
fierce by day, fierce by night,

most fierce

on the Ides when Caesar meets
his end.

Your pace begins to slow as
you approach
April,
named for your love,
Aphrodite,
Venus to your namesake.

You shed your battle gear,
your fierce
march diminishes
day by day, night by night,

as your softening
feet hope for an April affair.

A Dream about the Aquamarine

I dream the violent ocean
tosses me,
Odysseus
clinging
to a log—Poseidon's
rage forcing me to let go.

I breathe,
I swallow,
I cough to get the water out.

I die! I die! I die!

A mermaid hears my cough
above the roaring
tumble.

She swims to me with face
of worry,
takes an aquamarine
from her finger,
places it on mine, on mine.

Poseidon's rage calms.
I am no longer
Odysseus.

No longer do I dream.
I live! I live! I live! I live!

Folklore: Aquamarines are said to protect sailors while they are at sea. They also prevent sea sickness.

Ode to You O Daffodil

Daffadowndilly, daffydownlily,
daffodilly,
daffadilly, asphodel, affodel,
jonquil, narcissus—
all of these your names,
some given by serious botanicals,
some by silly humoranicals,
who say
the d is playfully added to affodel
to express the daffy way
you toss and dance
in the wind,
but I prefer the story the British
tell to show they
prefer
the imported asphodel
to you O native daffodil
by saying
you are the bastard 'affodel.

Pisces

Mighty Typhon shakes his
hundred heads
high
above the mountain cedars,
each open mouth
a howling furnace seeking
to devour an
arrogant Olympian god.

Angry Rhea, the Titan Queen,
created
him to rid the sky of upstart gods,
revenge
for banishing Cronos, the
Titan King,
from his short held   heavenly
throne.

Typhon approaches their
high
domain,
the twelve Olympian gods cringe
and begin to
morph into creatures
with power to fly,
or hide,
or speed along the ground,
or swim
in river, lake, or sea.

Aphrodite ties Eros, her son
to her,
foot to foot with cord and

jumps into the
sea,
turning into fish to
escape
the howling mouths.

Typhon, though, can
swim,
his fires turn the sea
to steam,
and just as he is
ready
to devour the pair,
her
son rises into the
air
on tiny wings, barely
lifting
both out of reach
for
Typhon cannot fly.

Before dawn
you may see them
tied tail to tail
by
that saving cord
in that part
of the sky called the sea.

The note on page 20 states that Gaea created Typhon. A variation of the myth states that Thea, Gaea's daughter, created Typhon.

A Clerihew for Robert Frost

Robert Frost
Deep in thought
Wrote the end could be fire or ice.
Would his surname suffice?

Van Gogh: *Starry Night*

The long brown swirls
from brush
that gentle touch the blue
and yellow
swirls
that are the starry night
are
the cedar

nature

unlike the sharp steeple
in the village
brushed
into
the swirling sky

steeple rising up
from
the place where things
are
made by man

artifact

cedar and steeple
each
trying to comfort a fevered sky

global warming

winter mountain melts
faster than ever
I've seen it before
into
rivulets
into streams
into rivers into
lakes that overflow

farther than ever
I've seen it before onto
what
used to be dry land

that swan on the mountain
side
shouldn't melt until
the middle
of April
but look it's gone

it's only the middle
of March

I say

only the middle
of March

winter mountain melts
faster than ever

I've seen it before
and next year? next year?

it's crazy warm
they say
it's crazy warm

it's global warming
they warn
it's global warming

and the government
ought
to do something
about it

make laws to slow it
they say
and
others say pray to God
pray
have the people at church
pray to slow it

but you and I know
that
government and churches
have no power
to slow it

for they bow
to
the global economy

bow
to

the global economy
let's make a secular
litany
a secular litany
I say

oh global economy help
us curb
the early
melt of winter mountain

oh global economy save
us from
the early
melt of winter mountain

I say

oh global economy prevent
the early
melt of winter mountain

for
it melts faster
than ever I've seen it before

pray for
us
oh global economy

"that swan on the mountain" — The swan made of snow high up on the western slope of the Grand Mesa outside Grand Junction, Colorado, is part of a Native American myth and part of a farmer myth. The farmer myth states that when the neck of the swan melts, separating head from body, it is time to plant.

on my seventieth

I'm beginning to feel
what it feels
to know
oblivion is only
a day
   a month
      a year
         ten perhaps twenty
away—
that moment from here to   ?

San Judas
para mi abuelita, Petrita Atencio

I saw mi abeulita standing on a chair
in the kitchen,
left hand propped against the wall, right hand
reaching up
onto the corner niche above her head,
fingers carefully
turning the statue of San Judas to the wall.

"¿Qué haces, abuelita?" I whispered softly,
afraid to frighten her.
"What are you doing? ¡Te vas a caer!
Why are you turning
the statue of San Judas to the wall?"

"Aye, Luis, I have lost patience con ese
santo. He won't
help me find my wedding ring.
I took it off to make
masa for the tortillas. It's been a week."

"But won't he get mad with his face
to the wall?"

"Luis, sometimes you have to put your
foot down!
Se va a cansar looking at the wall.
And I won't light
him any velitas until he finds my ring."

"Gramma, get off the chair. Here, let
me help you.
What if you fall? You'll get hurt
and have to
ask San José in the other corner to cure you."

59

I helped mi abuelita down. I told her
San Judas
would not be able to help her find the ring
with his face
turned toward the wall. She thought
about that
for awhile, then she said, "He knows
where it is,
he just wants me to light another velita.
I am not a rich woman. I cannot be

buying him
velitas every day. For a whole week
I walked into
the kitchen to see if San Judas had
been turned
around, but no, there he was with his
face to the wall.

Finally, I was in the kitchen when
abuelita went to
wash her apron and found the ring
in her pocket.
She turned her back to the back
of San Judas
and told me, "Luis, when I go outside,
turn San Judas
around slowly. I don't want him to
see where I found it.

San Judas is St. Jude, patron saint of lost things. San Antonio is the better known
patron of lost things. Velitas: votive candles.

"Beware the Ides of March"

"Beware the Ides of March," Mom and Dad
would have read had they
completed grade ten.

That may have made some impression
when I was born to them
that very day,

March 15, feast of St. Longinus who stabbed
Christ the King in the side while
on the cross.

They named me after him as was the custom
among Roman Catholics in
1938.

Longinus converted, was beheaded for Christ's
sake, was elevated to saint, Mom
and Dad

thinking that name a good omen for me.
They should have known there was
another stabbing

that day, the stabbing of Julius Caesar
because he would be king,
that one of his

assassins was named Longinus, Gaius Cassius
Longinus—if only they had
known

they might not have given me that name,
belonging to two Roman warriors,
and, by the way,

my middle name is Luis from the Latin
Ludovicus which means
warrior,

Longinus meaning lance or bearer of the spear,
and my surname Lopez meaning
son of the wolf.

How much more Roman can that be? If you
are famous and aspire to be king,
stay away from me,

"Beware the Ides of March!" Oh, I wish
my Mom and my Dad had
completed grade ten.

Shakespeare's Julius Caesar was commonly taught in the tenth grade curriculum.

Both Roman soldiers were centurions named Cassius Longinus. Longinus is
Latin for lance or he who carries a spear. The Longinus that pierced Christ as,
according to folklore, partially blind. Christ's blood cured him. When he
converted and was martyred, blood from his beheading cured the blind governor
who ordered his death.

be a talisman to me

     petrified water of the sea
     solid
     within with splendor
     yet
     changing
     as the sky changes
     be
     a talisman to me
     born
     this month and
     may
     hope and health be unchanging
     oh
     aquamarine

He Had That Something About Him

He had that something about him
that
made him like to do things like that.

When he was ten, he bought a kite,
paper,
sticks, glue, tail, all in one package.

The ball of white string he bought
separate.

Chose blue for the kite from a stack
of many colors.

Chose blue so he could hide the kite
in the sky.
Made people think he was flying string.

He had that something about him
That
made him like to do things like that.

When a stock boy at the grocery store,
he
filled empty bottles and cans with water,

labeled them "Heavier Fluid" and
placed
them next to cans of "Lighter Fluid.

One time at Catholic School he removed the
cross

from the outstretched hand of St. Ignatius
and
placed a can of Budweiser in its place.

When
in church he removed the baby Jesus
from the Virgin Mary's cuddling arms, put
a mirror
there so she could see her beautiful self.

He had that something about him
that
made him like to do things like that.

Tomorrow he will be eighty. I heard
him
say he misses doing things like that.

This morning I heard people say, "Did you see
that
old man flying string on the hill in the park?"

April

after Aphrodite
goddess of love
or
the Roman *aperire* to open
or
apes the bee

Diamond its gem
Sweet Pea the flower

under
Aries the ram

William Shakespeare
and
Leonardo da Vinci
born
        this month

upon her arrival

upon her arrival April signals
deep into each seed
the need
to feed forth a tendril of life

she
softens

she
caringly opens

each case
so life can twist out into her welcome

Diamonds

You say the Dresden sparkles
green,
Hope blue,
Cullinans colorless,
Saucy, Koh-i-Noor, and Nassak
too,
except for hints of brown.

You say
Tiffany glistens amber,
the Florentine a yellow-green.

I had always thought the diamond
colorless,
so you surprised me with this
diversity.

I am partial to green and amber,
but
I doubt
even in eternity
will I ever see
much less own a named one.

Lathyrus Odoratus (Sweet Pea)

Sweet Pea "sweet to the nose"
says
its botanical
"lathyrus odoratus"
and
certainly sweet to the eye
and
sweet to the feel of its petal
but
not to tongue or tummy
for
spastic paralysis and pain
are
the symptoms felt by those
who ingest
the
pea that is "sweet to the nose"

Aries

Aries leads the celestial twelve
Along the ecliptic,
Strong, regal in fleece of gold,
First to house the royal sun.

Aries is the lead sign of the Zodiac. The other eleven follow along the ecliptic.

Some Words from Shakespeare's Sonnet 33

All day these *basest clouds*
have ridden
your *celestial face,*
and now
at sunset *ugly rack* obscures
the blossom
I have so expected to enjoy.

I turn *forlorn* to walk away,
But out! alack!
the cloud
un*masks* ever so slightly,
so one,
then two, then three rays
make
the clouds fire into blossom.

Shakespeare's words italicized.

Leonardo's *St. Jerome*

What
was da Vinci thinking
when he painted

St. Jerome on one
knee
before a patch of
sunlit scratches on a cliff wall?

Are the scratches a temple
in a forest?

Is that his own face
looking
back
at him as from a mirror?

Is this a God sent vision?

Hard to tell.

With eyes intent upon the sunlit
patch,
left hand holding
his garment
close,

his right arm stretches out, holds
rock in fist
as if about to strike his bare
chest
in a *mea culpa*

or
about to throw
the rock at the seeming vision,

and
before him
at the foot of the painting,

a lion lies outstretched looking
up at him,
mouth
open as if to roar,

its tail encircling
a partially
buried human (Adam's) skull.

What was Leonardo thinking
when he painted

St. Jerome on one
knee
before a patch of
sunlit scratches on a cliff wall?

elm seed

listen to the skitter of elm seeds
on pavement
thousands gently rushed by morning breeze
across the parking lot to who knows where

to who knows where
and it gets me to thinking
which seeds will become
the elms that when mature
will scatter seeds
that skitter
on pavement
across parking lots to who knows where

political thoughts, April 2007

the President who loves
to
cowboy
it
over countries
and
sad to say
over us
is slipping off his horse

the saddle's loose

not many in
his posse
to help him tighten
straighten
since
one by one by one

they
have become the
objects
of other posses

some
headed for the hoosegow

Hoosegow is from the Spanish *juzgado*, meaning "having been judged"; therefore, here "cowboyed" to mean jail.

When I walked up to you

When I walked up to you
at the table,
you looked up,
your eyes,
surprised, welcomed me.

When I walked up to you
at the table,
you looked up,
your smile,
surprised, welcomed me.

When I walked up to you
at the table,
you looked up,
your shoulders,
surprised, welcomed me.

santa fe

una de las mujeres from our congregation
was brainwashed
by the moonies—she had those tendencies
porque
before that
she belonged to one of those Christian
flying saucer groups
and
before that
to one
of those "yo no se" agnostics
until
the people
who put hot stones
on your hurting places converted her—
but now
gracias a Dios
she is studying about Jesus in our seminary

"Santa fe" means "holy faith" in Spanish.

in April

water

f
a
l
l
s

from
the
sky

in
to

my

pa
t
i
o

and
plops

lit
tle
bu
bb   le

s
in

t
h
i
s

p   u   d   d   l   e

The Line between Love and Lust

Were Adam and Eve in love when they
partook of the apple?
I don't believe the Good Book tells us.

A serpent we read was the pander to lust,
but were they in love?

Perhaps love came after the lust, I simply
do not know.

I do know children were the result of later
partakings.

The line between love and lust is oh so thin,
I hope they were not in love when they first
partook.

I wouldn't want God to have died for a sin
oh so thin.

Perhaps the partaking was simply the bite
of the apple,
no literary symbol involved.

Then the serpent
was simply a pander to gluttony.

Am I too simple?
Would God
have had his Good Friday just for that?

To get out of this some say the act was
simple
disobedience.

How uninteresting.

May

for Maia
mother of Mercury

Emerald its gem
Lily the flower

looks up
at Taurus
and Maia's six sisters
the Pleiades

Dante Alighieri
and
Salvador Dali
born
            this month

Maia

I cannot help but rise to look
for you
in summer's predawn sky,
O Pleiades,
to wonder which of your diamond
stars is Maia
of the long lovely tresses,
tresses
that caught the eye of Zeus
as he
wondered at the beauty of each of you,
sparkling
wonders of the early morning sky.

It is Maia Zeus lured from sky
to cave,
it is Maia Zeus chose to bear
his trickster son,
and
it is Maia for whom this month
is named,
Maia,
loveliest among you, O predawn
diamonds,
Maia,
I, too, am in love with you.

The Pleiades, seven sisters, daughters of Atlas and Pleione, rise in Taurus
in the late June and early July predawn sky. Maia is one of the sisters.

i. q.

oh that I had owned
a emerald
in
my early years of scool

from what I here
just one small stone
set
in silver
and worn upon my finger
wood
have made my
i. q.
as good as eyenstines

To the Lily

Symbol of purity
you
are not allowed
to drop
your pollen upon the linen
on the Virgin's altar

Symbol of humility
you
do not mind
that
for that reason
your stamen is removed

Symbol of devotion
you
decorate the church
at the
Resurrection of her Son

Legend says
you
were with the
Virgin
at the foot of the Cross
three days before the Resurrection

Lovely oh lovely you
oh lily
Symbol of loyalty

Taurus

Taurus, what you are is evident,
who you are is not.
Are you the Cretan Bull captured
by Heracles?
Are you the bull in all its beauty
who carried off Europa?
Are you the brazen-footed bull Medea
helped Jason to slay?
Are you the reluctant bull who
was tricked
to lie with Pasiphae
and thus fathered the Minotaur?

It seems the who is something
to fear,
the red in your eye frightens me.

But since you carry the sisterly
Hyades,
and the somewhat sorrowful
Pleiades
On your neck and on your back,
I doubt
I need to fear your rushing at me.

Greek mythology is filled with the symbol of the bull. The constellation Taurus
can be understood as a number of bulls. Pasiphae, the wife of King Minos, fell
in love with a bull that would have nothing to do with her. Daedalus constructed
a wooden cow. Taurus loved the wooden cow, not knowing Pasiphae (the wife of
King Minos) was inside, resulting in the Minotaur. The star groups Pleiades and
Hesperides, daughters of Atlas, ride on Taurus's back, neck, or horns.

A Villanelle for Dante

The *Inferno* is more able than the Bible,
More forceful sure
Because Dante borrowed from Ovid most capable

Of teaching me that I am liable
For sin's mighty lure.
The *Purgatorio* is more able than the Bible.

It teaches that the wages of sin are payable
If only the sinner suffers to be pure
Because Dante borrowed from Ovid most capable

Of showing how the sinner's body is changeable,
Becomes tree, or bird, or boar.
The Paradiso is more able than the Bible

When it comes to arriving at Heaven's table,
Soul no longer impure,
Because Dante borrowed from Ovid most capable.

Dante teaches that measured bliss is attainable,
Ovid, perhaps, but I am sure
The Comedia is more able than the Bible
Because Dante borrowed from Ovid most capable.

L. Luis López
Salvador Dali: The Temptation of St. Anthony

At the bottom left of his dream, Dali painted St. Anthony, naked
in the desert, on one knee, strong legs, muscled back to me,
left arm behind him, hand placed solidly on rock, right arm
outstretched, makeshift cross in hand warding off a giant
rearing horse and five elephants, each

```
        o               s
        n               y
                        m
        s               b
        p               o
        i               l
        n               s
        d
        l               o
        y               f

        l               l
        e               u
        g               s
        s               t
```

balanced on their backs, a woman cupping her breasts
suggestively, another whose luscious bosom and lovely belly
show through golden castle windows,

```
        all             o
                        n
        w
        e               s
        i               p
        g
        h               i
        i               d
        h               e
        i               r
        n               y
        g

        d               l
        o               e
        w               g
        n               s.
```

90

I worry that St. Anthony might

d
r
o
p
t h e
c
r
o
s
s

and

for   embrace

reach   bosoms and belly

a   c
n   o
d   m
         e
a
l   t
l   u
       mb
w   l i
o   ng
u
l   d
d   own.

Between his legs Adam's skull stares up at him from the
desert floor, a warning to St. Anthony kneeling
and to Salvador Dali dreaming.

I Cannot Imagine

Can you imagine the night without
a Milky Way
or
the earth lacking fields of lilies white?

One night Zeus tricked Hera
into suckling
his mortal son Heracles
at her
lovely luscious breast,
had
Hermes place him so he could drink
her
immortal making milk,
but she, feeling the child's unfamiliar mouth,
pushed him away,
milk divine streaming out
among the stars,
some
falling to the earth like rain upon
lilies of the field
turning
them into oh so beautiful white.

Can you imagine the night without
a Milky Way
or
the earth lacking fields of lilies white?

upon meeting you

an unexpected breath of love blows soft
into my eyes
whispers into my heart
lingers
spirals down my body to my feet

then up
filling my every pore, sweetly residing
in my every thought
this unexpected breath of love blows soft

JUCO at Suplizio Field
for Sam Suplizio

Nothing is as pleasing to eye and heart
as a manicured baseball
field,
outfield
a green expanse
arching
from left to center to right,
crowned
by a rich brown warning track,
and that
by a fence of varied colors
stating in sections
that Brown Shoe Fit,
Alpine Bank,
City Market, KNZZ News,
KJCT TV,
Gene Taylor's Sporting Goods,
Wells Fargo,
and many, many more
support
Abner Doubleday's game.

Infield
a green diamond
crowned
again in brown,
home plate
and
three white bases at the corners,
while once more in brown
a raised circle patch
in the diamond's middle

sits
accented

by a small rectangle
called
the pitcher's rubber.

It is
in this place,
pleasant to eye and heart,
that
every May

crack of bat,
pop of glove, dugout chatter,
and
"C'mon blue"
will fill the manicured baseball park

at
JUCO
the Junior College World Series

JUCO, the Junior College World Series, has been played at Sam Suplizio Field in Grand Junction, Colorado, for fifty years. Sam was a former baseball player and businessman who was a force behind JUCO.

Imperfect Villanelle on an Imperfect War

Ah me! We lose our young citizens,
Mr. President,
Fighting the wrong, wrong enemy.

If they return, it's piece by piece,
Mr. Vice-President,
Ah me! We lose our young citizens.

Day by day in the streets of Baghdad,
Mr. Secretary of Defense,
We fight the wrong, wrong enemy.

Street by street and door by door,
Ms. Secretary of State,
Ah me! We lose our young citizens.

Land mines explode here, explode there,
Mr. Secretary of Defense,
We fight the wrong, wrong enemy.

Injured in body, injured in soul and mind,
Mr. Vice-President,
Ah me! We lose our young citizens.

Some return and some go back, back,
Mr. President,
Ah me! We lose our young citizens
Fighting the wrong, wrong enemy.

morning glory

a humming bit of rainbow
with a long beak
visits
a violet blossom
just as it
opens
to the warm slant of morning sun

the morning sun does bathe the bench

the morning sun does bathe the bench
does bathe the bench on which I work
on which I work this poem bright
this poem bright which does describe
which does describe the morning sun
the morning sun does bathe the bench

June

for Juno
Roman goddess queen

Pearl its gem
Rose the flower

beneath
Pollux and Castor the Gemini

San Juan de la Cruz
and
Diego Velásquez
born
                    this month

Mars to Romulus

Romulus,
my son, stand
tall
upon the Quirinal.
Cup
your hands,
call
to Greece,
summon Hera my mother,
bid
her be the goddess queen of Rome.
Say
Rome's most famous Caesar
will name her Juno,
name
this month for her.
Romulus,
Stand tall.
Call.
She will come.

to the teacher

from grain of sand to
pearl
in care of oyster shell

I send my child to
you
in hopes of cultured pearl

Ode to the Rose

Rosa pulchra—the beautiful rose,
nominative singular,
and
rosae pulchrae—of the beautiful rose,
genitive singular,
thus
Father Dardis drilled your Latin sound
into me,
made me memorize, memorize
dative, accusative, ablative,
vocative,
and
when done, of course, the plurals.

Rosa, of the family Rosaceae,
Dr. Cook in Botany termed you,
taught me to name your parts,
then
made me
memorize your myriad variations.

Symbol of love, passion, orgy,
Mary's virgin love,
Christ's blood,
and
Dante's grand Empyrean,
Miss Miller described you in literature.

And more:
vessel, yes, vessel for Shakespeare's

canker,
Blake's worm,
Burn's luve,
perfection in Dorothy Parker's mind,
the lily's mate in Campion's face,
and
"a rose is a rose is a rose" at Gertrude's pen.

I've heard
that if you ask the apothecary,
you are able to heal a mad dog's bite,
fill a barren womb,
treat the blues—

Rose!
Symbol of love, blood,
perfection, vessel for worm or canker,
and
remedy
for ill upon ill upon ill.

Rose!
Oh, Rosa Pulchra!
Thou art, thou art an education in thyself.

To Mo about the Gemini

Kin an egg come out of the womb,
Hatch a Pollux, hatch a Helena?
Kin the same time, same womb
Birth a Castor, birth a Clytemnestra?

Them ancient Greeks thought so.
What a strange tale they tell and tell.
Us cowboys don't have the market, Mo.
There's mo to this yarn I need to tell.

Zeus fathered Pollux and Helena on Leda
By turning into a swan.
Tyndareus fathered Castor and Clytemnestra
On Leda by being a husban'.

What a strange tale they tell and tell.
Better than Paul Bunyan or Pecos Bill.
That tale has sold and mo will sell,
Mo, than any cowboy tale will.

Here's mo. Pollux grew up to box,
Castor a tamer of horses.
Helena snuck off with Paris, that's the talk.
Clytemnestra killed her husban' say sources.

And yet mo, Mo. Pollux was divine.
Castor not.
Helena in beauty divine,
Clytemnestra not.

Pollux hankered to die after Castor was killed.
Begged Zeus to have his half brother

Share his immortality. Zeus that willed.
Put both Pollux and Castor as stars up there.

Now Helena is hated for startin' a war,
Her half sister lives in Hades,
A murderess murdered by her male ward.
Both gals in hearts drew the Queen of Spades.

So, Mo, when you look up at them stars,
See Castor and Pollux up there,
Remember that cowboys ain't got the market
When it comes to them Greeks back there.

In Greek mythology, Zeus falls in love with Leda. Leda refuses his advances, but he turns into a swan (the constellation Cygnus) and has Aphrodite (the constellation Aquila) chase him into Leda's arms. Zeus has his way with her (resulting in the twins Helen and Pollux), but she is already pregnant with her husband,s twins (Castor and Clytemnestra). All are born at the same time—stories vary. Castor and Pollux are known as the Gemini, a constellation of the Zodiac.

dark night of the soul
for San Juan de la Cruz

today my soul glooms gray
felt
remembrance of "My

God, my God

why

have you forsaken me?"

me

have you forsaken me if
you are,
and
that is the problem, are you?

at nine
of age I did not doubt,
now
I . . . now I . . . doubt,
no
I know you are not,

and

if you are not
no
reason for gloom

for gray in the soul

knowing I had no hand
in
killing you

so
why does not,
does not, does not my soul bloom joy?

To My Art Teacher about *vieja friendo huevos*
for Diego Velásquez

When I was only seven I thought
that painting
vieja friendo huevos
was about my grandmother
frying eggs
for me before school every morning.

I can see
it hanging on her kitchen wall.

She said
it reminded her of her love for me,
and it
certainly reminds me of my love for her.

But

you taught me to see it for what it is,
not about a grandmother
at all.

You said the painting was
by a young artist
proving
he could paint copper,
brass,
pottery,
glazed and unglazed,

straw, pewter, linen,
onion skin,
melon, wood, eggshell,
eggs in a ceramic casserole,
frying in stages
of opacity,
string,

a glass cruet with water,
eyes,
hand, young and old,

a nineteen year old
proving
himself a genius with paint and brush.

How my heart fell
when
you added the grandmother
and
the child
were only models,

and

that's when I noticed they
weren't even
looking at each other,

my heart falling.

But

upon thinking
about this, I don't think
Velásquez
will mind if I remember
it
as I saw it on my
grandmother's kitchen wall.

a.m. to p.m. (summer solstice)

seven
the tall desert rock catches
morning full face

its shadow yawns, stretches west

ten
its shadow disappearing into the rock

noon
its shadow deep inside asleep

two
its shadow emerging

four
its shadow stretches east

seven
the tall desert rock's turn to sleep

L. Luis López

Fajada Butte, If You Could Tell

Fajada Butte, you sit like a teller
of stories
looking over the mirage making heat
of Chaco Canyon.
I sit at this sheltered picnic table,
look out at you,
wonder
what stories you could tell
about the thousand
Junes
you have watched
since the days when a thousand
sweating bodies
built these kivas stone by stone,
smelled the aroma
of a thousand meals ground on metates
by kneeling women,
heard the beat
of a thousand drums in ceremony.
I turn my head and look down
the valley
into the mirages swimming
in the distance
and
realize
you could also reveal the mystery,
how and why
clan by clan by clan thousands
left
this valley,
burning kivas
until we have what we have,
a vast dry city,
isolated,

and
you could tell how all progressed
to my sitting
here
in the mirage-making heat of this afternoon.

to newlyweds

the sunflower follows
the sun
with radiant face
even
on cloudy day

flower the soul
of the lover
sun the one loved

flower the bride
sun the groom

groom the flower
bride the sun

each nourishes the other

yet the flower
is not the sun
the sun is not the flower

remember this on cloudy day

to Maggie

as dawn blushes
upon the valley mist,
your smile blushes
upon my misting heart

to the lightning bolt

multi-fork your instant being cracks
white into the cottonwood

arcing
half of it heavy to the ground

the shudder felt in my feet
then thunder

felt
in my shoulders rolling away, away, away

multi-fork your instant being cracked
white into the cottonwood

Sitting at a Table outside Starbucks

A man dressed in suit and tennis
shoes
pulls a child's wagon filled with
three
buckets of splashing water. The
wagon
has good wheels and
he
is pulling it along a nice
sidewalk,
but the sidewalk will end
down
the road and I wonder
how
far he is going and follow him
with
my eyes from my seat and
table
and vanilla latté. I decide
I
will finish my latté and
drive
after him in my pickup
to see where
he is going, and I see
him
pulling the wagon with splashing
water
along a dirt embankment.
Our
eyes meet and I go on in my
pickup, wondering, feeling
guilty,
and so I am writing this.

July

for Julius Caesar
self made god

Ruby the gem
Larkspur the flower

looking up
at Cancer the Crab

Pablo Neruda
and
Edgar Degas
born
                this month

Gaius Julius Caesar

for Gaius Julius Caesar become divine
this month is named,
Caesar,
who thrice
raised his palm
to push away the offered crown,
seeming
loath to have it,
Caesar,
pierced by knives
in palms
of those loathe to have him
be
their royal king,
Caesar,
who fell mortal
but
who, says Ovid, rose immortal
and
now rules this month in name over us.

Ruby

A beautiful bee   approached the ruby

hovered
          then
               des
                    cend
                      ed

trying to part   the ruby's starry light,

                    ed
                 cend
         as
disappointed

Oh beautiful bee,   the ruby is not for thee.

Larkspur

"Die!" cried Aias as he hacked
    at Odysseus
    and his men in battle rage,

"Ai!" cried Aias in his madness
    as he realized
    he was only killing sheep,

"Die!" cried Aias as in shame
    he turned
    the sword upon himself,

"Ai!" the words on the Larkspur
    petals
    born from the bloody ground.

Greek mythology says the Larkspur grew from Aias's (Ajax's) suicidal blood. It is also said that the word "Ai" can be read in the petals.

place is an illusion

solstice means the sun's stopping place
      on its journey north
tropic means the turn around place
      when the sun heads south

Cancer is the stop and turn place
      in summer
Capricorn is the stop and turn place
      in winter

in each case,
place is simply an illusion

star lore says my soul came to this place
      through Cancer
star lore says my soul will leave this place
      through Capricorn

where it comes from or where it goes,
      that place
      is simply another illusion

Today the Cancer turn around place is closer to Gemini, the Capricorn turn
around place is closer to Saggitarius.

A Question for Pablo Neruda

Will a child learning to walk
stand and fall, stand
and fall,
stand
and fall going from chair to couch
on
that planet with a sun like ours?

Pablo Neruda has a series of question poems like this one.

everything about the ballerina

everything about
the ballerina captured Degas
and
Degas captured everything about
the ballerina

with pencil, pen, pastel chalk,
and charcoal,
he moved among the dancers

then in his studio transformed
sketches
into glories of movement
of line of color

a ballerina stretching at the bar,
one
scratching her elegant back,
another
putting on her shoe,
and one
on toe, arms
graceful,
extended over her head,
hands
completing yet
hinting at the next move

observe
"Two Dancers at the Practice Bar,"
green tutus flowing,
feet placed
on yellow floor, legs
stretching
toward the orange wall

Oh! Degas captured everything about
the ballerina
and
everything about
the ballerina captured Degas

en el parque

pitching and batting en el parque
con su hijo,
cinco años
I would guess,
abuelito behind the plate
y
mamá con abuelita on the bench.

¡poom!

the ball rolls past papá chasing
it to the bushes,
mamá
cheering, "¡corre mi'hito, run!"
pero
abuelita "¡no pa' first!"
and
the boy corriendo quien sabe donde
y
abuelito taking credit for how to hit.

four old men

they cursed and spit and smoked
    roll-your-owns
they sat on a bench in front
    of the barber shop
they moved as slow as the revolving
    pole above them
four old men sitting in the shade
    in the heat of noon

watering the high desert

I sit and watch the sprinklers rotate
arcing rain high over the parched ground
giving promise to grass and weed

a sudden wind flings droplets in my
direction,
"Ah, so fresh the feel on hot skin!"

I wonder if some minister sitting in my
place preparing for Sunday pulpit
might find some message in all of this

Three Boys

Three boys at the flower
garden
watch two robins
land
near the hollyhocks.

One says, "Look!"
Another says, "How pretty!"
The third,
"But those are easy to shoot!"

Dream Vision for Langland and Chaucer

The high desert afternoon swelter
enters
my every pore,
makes my mouth dry,
eyes too hot to tear,
nostrils sere
from the heat of the rock I sit beside.

Nothing stirs,
I mean nothing stirs.
Lizard and bird are
nowhere seen.

Lethargic in body and mind,
I cannot think
to move from this torrid place,
wonder
why
the sun alone can . . . is that
a dog
I see, or is it a distant mirage?

I rub my eyes, the dog disappears.

With back to rock I pull upon the brim
of my hat,
shading my burning eyes
and fall asleep
then dream
I am looking down the dusty street
of a Western movie town
where a dog sleeps beneath a boardwalk

and I think
to lie beside the dog and die
in the heat
of these dog days of summer.

Dog days? With dog days in mind,
I think
to soothe my eyes in a second sleep and do.

In a second dream, a distant
bark awakens me
from one sleep then the other,
the bark sounding "dog!" "dog!" "dog!"
and
echoing "star!" "star!" "star!"
and
I remember what the ancients taught.
Sirius, the Dog Star,
lends its heat to the sun on days like this.

Now the rock is cooling,
ants and a lizard crawl about,
birds take flight,
and I
arise and walk away a learned man.

William Langland and Geoffrey Chaucer were writers of dream poetry during the
Middle Ages. They often described a dream within a dream.

Black Ant, Red Beetle

I watch the black ant drag the red beetle
five times its size
across
the sidewalk.
It seems to struggle and pull
in spurts,
seems to take a breath here and there.

Do ants have lungs and muscles that tire?

I am worried someone will come along,
step on both.
That would end the struggle.
I stand guard. The struggle goes on.

The ant approaches the edge of the sidewalk,
a cliff to it I would say,
and I wonder
how
it will get the beetle down the cliff,
as it seems
its weight will fall atop the ant,
but it simply repostions
its legs
and lets the beetle
hang
while it manages its way down.
If I had that many legs,
could I do something like that?

I lose sight of the ant and its burden.
It must have

entered a patch
of needles and cones near the sidewalk.

If the ant had a brain like mine,
I wonder if it could manage the red beetle.

August

named for Augustus
first emperor of Rome
another self made divine

Peridot its gem
Gladiola the flower

beneath
Leo's rule

Dorothy Parker
and
Andy Warhol
born
                    this month

Augustus Caesar

August should be named October
whether
you calculate by number
or
honor by name an emperor,
for
Augustus was Octavius,
the ordinal eighth,
and
by cardinal count October
is eight,
so
as you can readily see
August should be named October.

Peridot

That yellow-green gem on
your finger,
is that a peridot set in gold?

If so,
do you wear it to escape the terrors
of the night?

Or
do you wear it in fear of my cooking tonight?

In gem folklore, the peridot if set in gold and worn as an amulet has the powers
stated in the poem.

Gladiolus

If you give your love a gladiolus,
you give her the symbol
of splendid beauty,
but
be aware its name means sword
in Latin
and
"xiphion," its ancient name, means sword
in Greek.

Oh well,
the beauty
of love is often found in splendid danger.

Leo

The lion sun, mane aflame,
if it could roar,
the world
would
cringe in fear,
would
skip out of orbit,
and so would every planet to Pluto.

From sight of skipping Earth,
that other lion,
the constellation Leo,
would
no longer
softly pad across the sky
from east to west,
but
the lion sun,
mane aflame, would remain.

From a Certain Gentleman to "A Certain Lady"
for Dorothy Parker

What goes on when I'm away?
Oh! I can guess. Oh!
I can guess, dear Dorothy.

You present what you think
I want to hear
and see,
dear Dorothy—that
sweet smile, that
coquettish "tilt of head," that
lacy laugh that
seems to enjoy my made-up
"list of loves" I want to
impress you with,
even though I
sense you
die a "thousand little deaths."

You "kiss me blithely" as
I prepare to go,
but the smile I see is
for the places you plan to go.

Your mouth, soon to be painted
a "fragrant red," not
for me
but for someone else, begins

the first
of a "thousand little deaths"
within me—

dear Dorothy, Oh!
I need not guess
what goes on when I'm away.

This poem is in response to Dorothy Parker's "A Certain Lady." Lines from that poem are in quotation marks.

Campbell's Soup
a villanelle for Andy Warhol

Andy Warhol and I shared a love
Of Campbell's Soup.
Our mothers kept a treasure-trove

Of various kinds near the kitchen stove,
An array of soup
For which Andy and I shared a love.

Occasion determined which can of love,
Which can of soup
(For our mothers kept a treasure-trove)

They'd choose which could improve,
(Umm good that soup
For which Andy and I shared a love)

Would cure a cold or fill a stomach cove
Craving that soup
Of which our mothers kept a treasure-trove.

Andy made famous a mother's love
By painting Campbell's Soup.
Andy Warhol and I shared a love.
Our mothers kept a treasure-trove.

centipede

as my feet touch the floor
this morn
and I steady myself
for the walk
to the washroom, I notice
a centipede
making its way up the wall
its tiny brain managing
one hundred
while mine can barely manage two

Meditation

I awoke into a dream

the face of God staring at me from
the southeast sky,
mouth open wide in wonder, just before
the sun began to rise

I said a prayer

at ten
his open mouth drew wide in anger
I began to wonder what I had done

I said a prayer

at three
his mouth drew down in sorrow
I felt shame for what I do not know

I said a prayer

at six
the face of God stopped staring at me from
the southeast sky,
his lips smiled slightly, I said Amen

from my dream, I slipped into sleep

Russian Olive

Russian Olive, the breeze plays
with your leaves,
sometimes
silver, sometimes green,
reminding me
of the state of my Olive's ways.

Search for Life

I'm having trouble with this poem.
I think it's dead.

I might settle for seeming life.

Five-fifty in the morning.

Birds chirp here and there
in the canyon,

dart from bush to branch of
dead piñon,

momentary leaves perching

nervously,

fluff themselves,
give seeming life to the dead tree.

I, a momentary visitor,
in search of life to give life
to this poem,
sit outside my tent,
hands around a hot cup of coffee,
suddenly see that
dart and chirp and fluff of bird

gives seeming life to tree and poem.

Campground

This morn
I watch Dawn apply her makeup,
Preparing
For Helius. He will soon awaken.

Convenience

What used to be home and grocery
for
deer, birds, bugs, and fish
has
been turned into a grocery
for
people, people, people, people, people.

Drainage experts have
invaded
this wetland place,
machines
have yanked trees and
machines
have dug dirt and pushed
bush
from place to place, and
those
with hammers, saws, and measuring
tapes
have frightened off the denisons
that
used to live and shop
here.

I guess the hind end of the
Superstore
will be just as beautiful
as
bush and tree, and trash
bins

just as eyecatching as
rows
of cattail beside the stream,
and
the pretty winged birds as
satisfied
with parking lot pickings
as
I will be with sound of starting
cars
and honking horns
instead
of sound of running water.

I'll miss my morning walk in the
wetlands,
but, oh well, I'll be able to
get
my quart of milk, cup of
coffee
and sugar donut with dispatch.

September

the ninth month
mislabeled the seventh

Sapphire its gem
Aster the flower

looks up
at Virgo's sheaf

Miguel de Cervantes Saavedra
and
Michelangelo Merisi de Caravaggio
born
                        this month

Put Them Romans in Very Hot Embers

Put them Romans in very
hot embers
for not renumbering
the last four months
of the year when they
made the Julian Calendar.

Place there Pope Gregory
since he could have
made the correction

but didn't—oh, September
would be November,
October December,
November Undecimber,
December Duodecimber,

the last two being eleven
and twelve in Latin—oh
make them embers even
ever hotter
for making me write this.

Decem is ten in Latin. When a prefix is added, the word becomes decim. The
added ber comes from an assimilation of the Latin word for month, mens and
membris (see Random House Dictionary), so that I make up the words Undec-
imber (eleven) and Duodecimber (twelve) as possible new names for November
and December.

The Ten Commandments

You say heaven delivered the
Ten Commandments
To
Moses on tablets of sapphire.

You say this gives immediacy
To
Thou shalt and thou shalt not.

How intriguing!
Isn't that your birthstone?

I guess you know that the
Sapphire loses
Luster
When worn by spouse unfaithful!

Jewish folklore tells the story the tablets and sapphire.

hope in the face of fearful winter

the aster blooms its stars
in autumn,
waves farewell to summer, warns
of winter yet
foretells the following spring

because in bloom on the archangel's
day,
called the michaelmas daisy,
St. Michael and
the Aster,
hope in the face of fearful winter

September 30 is the Feast of St. Michael, Michaelmas Day.

Virgo

As I talk, my green laser pointer
follows a curve
in the handle of the Big Dipper
sort of south
to Arcturus in the knee of Bootes,
continues
south to the star of stars
in Virgo, Spica,
which marks the sheaf of corn
in her left hand,
moves west to her head,
east down
the right side of her body
to the palm frond
in her right hand, then further
to her feet.

"Virgo represents a number of famous
women," I say
as I turn off my lazer. "Among
the Greeks she
is Persephone stolen by Hades
from a field
of flowers, or Erigone, daughter
of Icarius,
who is Bootes, or Astraea if one
includes the scales
of Libra at her feet, or Ishtar
among the Babylonians, Astarte
or Eostre
among the Angles and Saxons, Kanya
the mother of Krishna,

or among Christians,
the Virgin Mary holding her child.

I am tempted to tell the story
of each,
but feel I will lose my audience,
so I ask
"Are there any Virgos in the group?"

A young lady
raises her hand hesitantly,
and I say,
"Virgos are absolutely neat, orderly,
critical,
excellent mathematicians, and precise
scholars."

Virgo, in a tentative voice, says
"I think
the one about the Virgin Mary
is correct
because I think it is somewhere
in the Bible."

My laser flicks on and moves
to the
question mark in the face of Leo.

Salvador Quintana
for Miguel de Cervantes Saavedra

When on his meds, Salvador Quintana
leaves Rosy his Chevy
in the garage, walks to, sits
at McDonalds,
drinks coffee, eats apple pie, smokes
a cigarette,
drinks coffee, eats cherry pie, smokes
a cigarette,
drinks coffee, eats apple pie, smokes
a cigarette.
Salvador Quintana when on his meds.

When off his meds, Salvador Quintana
takes Rosy his Chevy
out of the garage, drives to, sits
at Joe's Bar,
drinks wine, eats chips, smokes
a cigarette,
drinks beer, eats peanuts, smokes
a cigarette,
drinks whiskey, eats sausage, smokes
a cigarette.
Salvador Quintana when off his meds.

But this was not always Salvador Quintana.
Before he was twenty
he played center field for the Gold Sox,
drew cartoons,
made people laugh and laugh when
he mimicked
Cantinflas, Jerry Lewis, sang
like Dean Martin or Little Richard,

loved to dance,
had his Dulcinea deep in his heart, had
marriage in mind.
This before twenty was Salvador Quintana.

But his Dulcinea chose another,
Dulcinea chose another,
she chose another,
chose another.

Purity of love began to decay deep in his
heart, anger festered deep
in his brain,
voice upon voice upon voice arose,
unleashing word upon word,
talking all at once, all at once, until

something snapped, snapped
in his head. He saw giants whirling
on the horizon,
saw fearsome knights
riding out of the dark, dark woods,
heard from the voices
that acid licked from the back of stamps
would make the giants
friendly,
heard that sips
of red liquid from the bottle
would make fearsome knights
riding out of the dark, dark woods kindly.

I have known this Salvador Quintana
forty years,
I knew the other Salvador Quintana
before he was twenty.
I saw the change from that Salvador Quintana

to the present Salvador Quintana.

Today Salvador Quintana and I will
leave Rosy his Chevy
in the garage, we will walk to, then sit
at McDonalds,
drink coffee, eat apple pie, smoke
a cigarette,
drink coffee, eat cherry pie, smoke
a cigarette,
drink coffee, eat apple pie, smoke
a cigarette.

It's Salvador Quintana's birthday.
I will
celebrate with my brother on his sixtieth.

The Death of the Virgin (1601) by Caravaggio

Michelangelo Merisi de Caravaggio, what
prompted you to use your beloved prostitute
as a model
for the dead Virgin Mary, Mother of God?

There she lies, outstretched in red, right hand
placed just below her breast, left arm stretched
over the bed,
hand hanging over the edge, head slightly left.

Michelangelo Merisi de Caravaggio, what
prompted you to use your beloved prostitute
as a model
for the dead Virgin Mary, Mother of God?

The Virgin Mary's body seems swollen. Is she
in rigor mortis? A brown cover lies across
her lower body,
but her bare feet are exposed. Is this undignified?

Michelangelo Merisi de Caravaggio, what
prompted you to use your beloved prostitute
as a model
for the dead Virgin Mary, Mother of God?

To her right and above you positioned grieving
apostles in a vee, hands hiding sorrow in their faces,
at her feet,
over her right hand, at her head, bowing over her.

Michelangelo Merisi de Caravaggio, what
prompted you to use your beloved prostitute
as a model
for the dead Virgin Mary, Mother of God?

Light shines down from the upper left upon heads,
shoulders, hands, upon the Virgin Mary's
upper body,
on the bare feet of the Virgin dead upon her bed.

Michelangelo Merisi de Caravaggio, what
prompted you to use your beloved prostitute
as a model
for the dead Virgin Mary, Mother of God?

In the foreground, light falls upon the back
of the seated Mary Magadalene, shoulders bent
forward in sorrow,
left arm supporting her head upon her lap.

Michelangelo Merisi de Caravaggio, what
prompted you to use your beloved prostitute
as a model
for the dead Virgin Mary, Mother of God?

Caravaggio, this is the Mother of God, purity
personified. Didn't her Godly Son take her to
heaven alive? You
painted her dead, Mary, with no hint of heaven.

Michelangelo Merisi de Caravaggio, what
prompted you to use your beloved prostitute
as a model
for the dead Virgin Mary, Mother of God?

The monks at Santa Maria della Scalla who
commissioned the painting, recognized your
beloved prostitute.
No wonder they rejected the painting in grief.

Michelangelo Merisi de Caravaggio, what
prompted you to use your beloved prostitute
as a model
for the dead Virgin Mary, Mother of God?

September Eleven

September Eleven changed the world
they say

Osama believing he had struck victory
for his God

that day

given as chance for all who follow
Christ

to say to Osama as Christ said on that
painful cross

"Father, forgive them for they know not
what the do"

but I fear that may not have crossed any
Christian leader's mind

how would that have changed the world
would you say?

Stopping by Sign 18: Pinyon Pine
(Pinus Edulis)

Is this the pine that grows piñón,
the pine we spread the sheet beneath and shook
to get nut and cone when I was young?
Looks like it as I remember.
But pinyon (pín-yahn)?
I don't recall that spelling or pronunciation.
Piñón (peen-yóhn).
That's what I remember.

Y me acuerdo de mis cousins,
mis tíos, tías, hermanos, hermanas,
abuelo, abuela, mamá, papá, all of us
getting las manos sticky
as we gathered piñón not pinyon.
Pinyon?
Do they roast as well with a name like that?
Ah, the roasting! Aroma from heaven!
And the taste? ¡Aye Dios, delicioso!

Piñón, pinyon, pine nut,
pinyon pine nut, nut pine, and more
appear in dictionaries.

The Colorado National Monument Guide
reads piñón.
A chiropracter's sign reads pinyon.
A recipe in the
Rancho de Chimayo Cookbook reads piñón.
The poetry magazine
at Mesa State College reads Pinyon.

I'm not done.

I looked up pinus edulis.
It's Latin
for eatable or edible pine.
Eatable
if you want to flaunt your Anglo-Saxon.
Edible
if you want to flaunt your Latin.

And, oh yes, what we buy at the store
in packages
comes from China.
They're given the Italian name Pignolia.

All this from stopping
At Sign 18: Pinyon Pine (Pinus edulis). Pinyon?

Piñón is traditionally harvested in September in the Southwest United States.
The harvest and the roasting are often an extended family affair.

My Brand: A Cowboy Poem

Three L's my brand were I to have
One made for me.
"How duh yuh want them L's to behave?"
The blacksmith sez to me.

"What kin I have?" I sez to him.
"Three L's in a row,"
Sez he, "under a roof. Fat or slim.
Bar above. Bar below.

Inside a circle. Inside a square.
Three L's slant.
Now that would be mighty rare,"
His fingers do a little dance.

"I like the dance," sez I. "Make 'em slim."
My thumb and index
Finger showin' just how thin.
"What about the letters?" he sez.

"Ya want them L's block or cursive?"
"Cursive would be nice,"
I sez, and he, "That would be a massive
Headache, the price

Pretty high." "Tell ya what," sez I,
"Make 'em block,
Don't let 'em dance, one bar high,
One low," No more talk,

Cuz my eyes are lookin' for the John.
"Wait," he sez, voice
And fingers holding me up, "One
More little choice.

Upper case or lower case?" he asks,
But oh I'm desperate,
"Lower, but, but where's the John?" I ask.
He, in a deliberate

Drawl, his fingers slowly talkin'
Sez, "Three slim, block, low
Case l's in a row, not dancin'
Bar above, bar below."

"Yes," sez I, my eyes beggin' for the men's,
"With that I agree!"
His talkin' fingers slowly point the direction.
In a flash, I flee.

One week later, the blacksmith calls,
"It's done, come see."
I do. But the brand's not mine at all.
It's the Roman numeral III.

so I left him fuming

why do you come here from that South
saying y'all
and not hardly speaking no Spanish
my Dad says

you went away speaking good English
and good Spanish
and
now you come here with y'all and
down the holler instead of alla
or over there
and I say Dad I just like
to talk like where I am

so now I will say ese and alla
and to get more on his
nerves said cómo esta usted y'all
mon pere because I spent part
of my South in Louisiana
among the Cajuns

and he said I mean he really
said nada and lit a Chesterfield
and that meant he said nada
even more—so I left him fuming

The Naming of Time

As smart as we think we are,

Why let September
be
number nine, October number ten?

Why did we not correct
when
adding June and July?

We send rockets to Jupiter,
map our own DNA,
and clone a bleating sheep.

Why not correct the naming of time?

Tycho, Kepler, Newton, Einstein
lived this error.
Perhaps this poem will instigate change.

Well, though I've made
some noise,
I sort of hope not.

Arrogance can stand such
imperfection
to cure how smart we think we are.

the picket fence

sunbleached splintered pickets
      hanging by rusty nails
      to what is left

ancient broken men
      hanging by heart beats
      to what is left

October

Octo means eight
but
this is month number ten

Opal its gem
Marigold the flower

beneath
Libra's scales

Rome's Virgil
and
Spain's Pablo Picasso
born
        this month

A Limerick for October

I can hardly wait for October
For then the German beer flows over
    And I sit and I sip
    Holding mug to my lips
At the inn called Aye Bee Sober.

Opal

Opal, thy name is simply stone,
but
you are rainbow to the eye,
containing
the glory of all precious stones,
such glory,
hallelujah, hallelujah, hallelujah!

Ode to the Marigold

As often as I kneel before Mary's altar,
I see you here
ever present before her carvéd feet,
every month of every year,
almost.
You are Mary's gold, you grow from seed
to stem to flower
to adorn her image, but for
a tiny time at Easter
when
the white lily takes your place.
Did you know
the Church as chosen the lily
as Mary's flower?
What?
I disagree!
In my mind you are the faithful flower,
Mary's gold.
I want only you at her carvéd feet.

Libra of the Zoo-diac
How we changed the sky and got things wrong.

The stars that make up Libra,
were they not
pincers that belonged to Scorpio?

Were they not the scales that belonged
to Dike as she
placed deeds just, unjust in respective pans?

Were they not the scales that belonged
to apotheosized Caesar
commissioned
before his death on Roman coins?

Yes, yes, and yes, but we ruined the
Zodiac when we
detached animal and human, leaving only
the mechanical—no one holding the scales.

Libra,
you are not like others in the Zoo-diac.

As members of the zodiac, Capricorn, Cancer, Scorpio, Pisces, Taurus, Leo, and Aries are animals. Aquarius, Gemini, Virgo, and Sagittarius are humans. Only Libra is mechanical. The "zo" in zodiac means animal.

encounter with La Llorona upon his return from Harvard

for Virgil

late October's moonlight
chill casts
a gray-white mist
upon the day's
vibrant red and gold
of brush
along the river's banks

like an Aeneas
he stands
at the edge of Tartaros
expecting to see Chiron
standing silently
in his boat beckoning to those
who would cross
holding
his boney hand out
for the penny

like Aeneas
he thinks of turning
to Sybil for protection
from the hidden
crouching three-throated dog

not since he
was ten had he walked
this way on Halloween
and never alone

for he had heard it said
that those souls
whose bodies were never
retrieved
from the river's bottom
that lie entangled

in roots along the river's edge
haunt these banks
called forth
by the moon's eerie chill

he does not know
what called him here
or why he came alone
for he knew that anyone
who happened
upon a soul rising from
the river is rooted
to the bank
must observe hideous
transformations
is in danger of losing his soul

he tried to turn
and run from that place
but too late
for a mist spiraled
from the river's surface
an El Greco figure
elongating towards the moon

clouding it
becoming the face of a woman
in pain
hollowed eyes
and wailing mouth

the moon
becoming two
a cold pupil in each hollow
staring

directly into his own
searching
for his soul
trying to suck it forth

in that moment of panic
he remembered what
the old one's taught
about fighting off these
restless souls

he forced his eyes shut
and cried out

"Señora I am not yours

your children
have long been swept away
though their souls
may wander
somewhere along the shore

"Señora I am not yours"

the pull subsided
as the mist's chill grip
released him

he opened his eyes
and
saw only hollows
where
the moon's had been

the mist
uncovered the moon
and
spiraled down
shortening in length
until it returned
to the river

leaving him alone

La Llorona is the weeping woman looking for her drowned children along river
and ditch banks in Southwest Hispanic stories.

picasso as a baby

"piz, piz" for lapiz, his pencil, "sus
primeras palabras,"
his mother said, for he wanted
to draw
torruellas, whirl upon whirl, with his
tiny hands,
then
"suca" cakes,
"suca" cakes
he called them in his tiny talk

"sus primeras palabras" ("his first words"). Picasso wanted to draw swirls (torruellas) that indicated sugar cakes.

Autumn

The chilling wind is putting out
Cottonwood flames
Along the stream,
Not all at once,
But leaf by leaf,
Thousands of votive candles
Blown out one by one
In preparation for dark winter.

October Workshop

The ladies sit here and there
on the lawn,
nine in all,
taking in
the mid-morning river,
cottonwoods, and mountain cedars beyond.

This evening
each retreats to pad and pencil.

In the morning we will share
nine
inspirations
drawn from this morning's yellow display.

To My Fundamental Friend about the Moon

The old story tells me that
the moon is Hecate
in the underworld, Artemis
in the new crescent,
Selene in the full, Artemis
again in the reverse
crescent
and Hecate in the underworld.

That's the old story, but I do
know the earth's
rotation,
the moon's attitude toward the earth,
the sun's shine,
what may have made the moon,
the why of craters
on its face.
That's the new story.

And you know what?
I learned both stories in school.

I learned about the moon
in mythology.
I learned about the moon
in astronomy.

In one I learned about how humans
use the heart.
In the other I learned about how humans
use the brain.

Oh, but you, my friend, are
not listening.
You are ready to tell me
who made it.

Please Don't Run From Me

I do love you,
please don't run from me.
I won't hurt you,
please don't run from me.
I want to ask,
please don't run from me,
if you do know,
please don't run from me,
how much I love,
please don't run from me,
to have
you run from me.

Halloween Haiku

A knock at the door,
Three skeletons, bags in hand,
Beg for treats to eat.

October 2006

The urgent buzz disturbs my dream,
my warm hand
reaches out from beneath
warm covers
searching for the click that stops the buzz
but finds
the telephone instead.

I sit up and dial in the dark.

"Dad, they're in! The Cardinals!
They're in! Against Detroit!
The World Series! Can you believe it?
We'll watch together. I'll bring the Bud!"

Through the disturbing buzz
a woman's soft voice,
"Sir, I believe you have the wrong number."

"Is this 246-4646?"
"Yes."
"What are you doing with my Dad's number?"

A frightened click awakens me.
I grope for the light switch.
"Click!"
Reach to quash the blatant buzz
then
notice the phone sitting quietly in its cradle.

Had I dialed Dad from my dream,
my Cardinal fan Dad who lived
the last inning of his life this day 1986?

This afternoon I sit at
Traders Coffee and Tea, daydreaming
over a vanilla latte.
Dad takes the chair across from me,
stirs cream and a heaping spoon of sugar
into his steaming
coffee, sips, then leans
forward, "Son, thanks for letting me know."

November

wrongly numbered nine
really number eleven

Topaz its gem
Chrysanthemum the flower

fearing
Scorpio's sting

Robert Blake
and
Georgia O'Keeffe
born
                  this month

Birth of November

You are born each year from frightful
pains of October,
her labor
that last night filled
with ghouls, ghosts, goblins, witches,
devils, and skeletons
that walk the streets, approach
neighborhood doors, and threaten trick
or treat
until they begin to
disappear
at dark
into their homes, leaving
the night
serene
until you are born
into the Day of Saints
between the tick and the tock of midnight.

Topaz

The topaz gem when color of fire
warms the hand,
warns
through change in shade
of poison
in food or drink, and
when
ground to powder and stirred
in drink,
relieves the sick, cures death.

Some call it the Hyacinth stone.
Why? I don't know.

Folklore says whoever wears
the stone is made
invisible when
danger approaches.

Alas! Hyacinth was not wearing
the topaz
when Apollo let go the errant disc,
but then we
wouldn't have the Hyacinth flower.

Apollo, throwing the disc in an athletic contest, sent it awry, thus killing Hyacinth, his lover. In the place where his blood was shed, grew a flower, named by Apollo the hyacinth flower.

God's Eyebrow

Chrysanthemum, gold flower,
folks call it
God's Eyebrow, when made into
garlands,
protects against demons.

I can see his Eyebrow raised
in warning,
not once but in profusion,
sending
hosts of demons in confusion.

I tend to sneeze when near
the Chrysanthemum,
but I don't have to worry about
being alone,
someone not saying, "God Bless You,"
since his Eyebrow
will keep at bay any demon
who tries
to replace my sneezed out soul.

To Scorpio

Mother Earth sent you
to sting Orion
on the heel,
kill him, cure the
Mighty Hunter's proud
attempt to rid the
earth of every wild beast.

But, Ophiucus, centaur-
taught healer,
cured Orion of death,
crushed your head
with his heel,
ground it
deep into Mother Earth.

Hades complained
Ophiucus
would rid his realm of
future citizens,
so Zeus struck him
with a thunderbolt,
the giver
of life gave up his life.

Now you, Scorpio,
with
Orion and Ophiucus, are
in the sky.
You rise in the east
to chase
Orion, but he descends

into the
west. Ophiucus has his
foot
firmly on your head.

Scorpio, being obedient
to
Mother Earth,
you deserve more than this.

Ophiucus, a summer constellation, is the serpent bearer. His alternate name is
Aesclepius, the Greek and Roman god of healing.

"What Are You Saying, Mr. Blake?"

"What are you saying, Mr. Blake?"
Does God *smile his work to see?*

He made the *Little Lamb*
meek and mild.
He framed the *fearful* Tiger
burning bright.

He called himself *by* the name
of the *Lamb,*
and then He blessed it *meek* and *mild.*

He did not name himself by the
Tyger's name.
He did not *bless* that *fearful* might.

God, it seems, Mr. Blake, named
himself *meek* and *mild,*
made the *Lamb* his human self.

Had he made himself the *Tyger's*
fearful might, we would fear
his *dread hand,* his *dread* feet.

If I imitate him *meek* and *mild,*
and not the *Tyger's fearful might,*
will God then *smile his work to see?*

Italicized words from "The Lamb" and from "The Tyger."

To Georgia O'Keeffe in Spanglish

Querida Georgia,

Este painting of la escalera to la luna,
may be about your dream,
pero también it is also about la mía.

the ladder floating upright en el cielo
between the far up half luna waxing
and the muy abajo silhouette
of la montaña que se llama Pedernal,

is as I look at it about me.

Eight rungs form seven spaces, cada
space, en años, a decade.

Yo ready to step to the seventh,
have climbed mi vida
rung by rung by rung by rung by rung by
rung, and soon another.

My life feels light having lived what I
have lived en esta
escalera.
I will join you when I step from
the eighth, you

having stepped beyond towards la
media luna waxing
where a ninth should be en la escalera.

So you see, when you painted the ladder,
you painted both of our dreams.

Con mucho cariño,

Luis

my lonely ark
a triolet

my lonely ark, a speck on the deep,
    is pressed against the sky
where I hear helpless Noah weep,
my lonely ark, a speck on the deep,
so forlorn, I too weep;
    praying for an Ararat, I cry
my lonely ark, a speck on the deep
    is pressed against the sky

Nonsense?
Three Limericks

There was a bearded man from Spain,
Hernán Cortez his name, to Aztecs a bane,
    They thought him Quetzecoatl
    Their sun God returned after some while,
A God indeed, he pillaged to give his God gain.

Cortez and his men, spreaders of smallpox,
Killed thousands of Aztecs, then rose a paradox.
    Cortez was horrified by evidence
    Of human sacrifice he thought maleficent,
Burned temples, killed Aztecs, thought himself orthodox.

But before you put too much blame on Cortez,
You need to know Aztecs took from Toltecs,
    Toltecs took from Mayan,
    Mayan invaded whomever in Yukatan,
Each believed in the hereafter—which will that possess?

With Thinning in Mind

Once again I stand before my bookshelves
with thinning in mind.

This time I have planned oh so carefully.
three empty boxes

sit at the foot of the bookshelves, one for
throw away, one

for student or friend giveaway, and one
for library donation.

They wait for what I decide will be
quick decisions,

keep it, box one, box two, box three. But
as I eye then touch

each book, it speaks inside my head,
"When that Aprille

with his shoures. . . ." A keeper, then
"Midway on my

life's journey. . . ." Another keeper, so
I skip to another

shelf where Paul Horgan's *Great River* sits,
"There was no record
but memory and it became tradition

then legend

and then religion." Yes, I remember.
I need to revisit.

And, oh, here's Momaday. "There was a house
made of dawn.

It was made of pollen and of. . . ." Who was
the main character?

So I move to another shelf where Plato
beckons, enticing

me to sit with Socrates and Euthyphro.
Then Homer and Hesiod call

upon their muses, then to another
shelf where

"Batter my heart three-personed god. . . ." resounds,
and to Rudolfo Anaya

who interrupts with, "Ultima came to stay with us
the summer

I was almost seven." I'm supposed to prepare
a paper on Ultima.

And look, *Italian in 10 Minutes a Day.*
Maybe now I have time. . . .

Two hours later boxes sit empty at the foot
of my bookshelves.

So much for thinning. Well, I'll keep the boxes,
just in case.

so shy

the day moon faces
three quarter
through
the branches of that winter tree

she's a gem
set to flirt with me

but

as with any woman
I turn
my frightened bashful face away

Ssssh!

Amazing how much noise
one person
can make in the quiet of a library.

I remember the turning
of pages,
the scratch of pen on paper,
clearing the throat,
the shifting in and the scrape
of chairs,
whispers,
a sneeze,
the accompanying "Bless you,"
and the
occasional drop of a book.

Ssssh!

"Be glad," I'm told
for now
it's the little tune
as one connects to Microsoft,
the cell phone ring,
the hushed, "Hello,"
and the loud
repeat, "I can't talk now, I'm
in the library."

Ssssh!

Cardboard Cell Phone

He's in line at the coffee counter, homeless,
he seems,
greasy Boston baseball cap,
shoddy shoes,
rope for belt,
out of place in this line of cell phone
glued-to-ear customers.
One a well-dressed lady at the front
of the line,
"Yak, yak, tall, yak, yak, latte, vanilla,
sugarless, yak, yak, skim,
yak, oh, extra hot, yak, yak!"
Card through
the little machine, "Yak, yak, yak!"

Finally next to order,
the homeless man sings out,
"La Donna e Mobile, La Donna e Mobile!"
from Rigoletto,
reaches into his left hip pocket,
pulls out
a palm-sized piece of cardboard,
pulls up
on his Boston cap,
holds cardboard to ear,

"It's Simon,
can't talk now,
I ain't yet had by bleepin' mornin' joe!"

Then, when the coffee girls asks,

"Oh, grande, dark roast, three
fingers for cream," he says

to her,
then into the phone,

"What? No, I ain't goin' to buy her no joe!"

When it comes time to pay,
I sense trouble.
The coffee girl says, "That'll
Be $1.56, please," like she's not going to get it.

He reaches into his right hip
pocket,
pulls out a rumpled wad
of bills,
"An' I ain't buyin' her no smokes neither!"
tosses it
on the counter,
"Take what you need and keep the rest."

"We're not allowed to take tips, Sir."

"Well hell!" he says to
her and to the
someone in the cardboard phone,
"One
wants my money,
the other
won't take it! I don't need
no woman an' I don't need no joe!"
he yells into his phone,
flips it into his hip pocket,
pulls down
on his Boston cap,
and scuffles out in shoddy shoes.

December

the twelfth labeled
the tenth

Turquoise its gem
Narcissus the flower

under
the bow and arrow of Sagittarius

Emily Dickenson
and
George Seurat
born
                    this month

December 1980
This poetic note on my Beowulf term paper

Luis,

I sit here sullen   in my study,
Watch it snow   outside my window
Big, beautiful   fluffy flakes,
Cup of coffee   creamy, steaming
On my desk   next to a double
Pile of bulky   Beowulf papers,
Bent to grade   both piles by two.

But yours sits   open before me.

I sip my coffee   swallow slowly,

Then pencil poised   drop point
To paper where   I write, "Not
All snow falls   outside my window!"

             Your grade—C-
             Dr. Ellen Curren

The above is an Anglo-Saxon alliterative style poem. See *Beowulf.*

Turquoise

Wearing sky blue or green,
I understand,
when set as a gem
brings
booty to the warrior,
the hunted to the hunter,
happiness
and good fortune to all.

Let not
prelates and politicians
know this.

Narcissus

your beauty, Narcissus, stares
at you
from the still water of the pond,
stares
with astonished love
until
sudden arms reach
up
to embrace you,

the water-mirror moves
in wrinkles

then stills,

as a yellow flower
grows down
into the pond, there at the
edge
grows down into the pond,

that, now your beauty, Narcissus

To Sagittarius

For all your wild, lusty centaur play,
often galloping
in drunken abandon,
angry
when drinking the fruit of the trodden
grape,
bow and arrow aimed at the fearful
scorpion,
when you are pointed out to me,
are merely
a teapot,
your steam making up the Milky Way.

The configuration of this constellation can be seen as a centaur with bow and arrow or as a teapot.

Thank You Emily Dickenson

"Tell all the truth but tell it slant,"
Wrote Emily Dickenson,
And in stanza two,
"The Truth must dazzle gradually
Or every man be blind."

Tell many a lie but tell it slant,
The art of many a politician,
Except that slant becomes spin to woo
The mind to think dazzling Lie is Truth
Confusedly, so "every man be blind."

From Emily Dickenson's poem "Tell all the truth but tell it slant - " 1263 (1129)

A Child Discovers
The Dots Made Famous by Georges Seurat

The comic book lies on the kitchen table,
Captain Marvel in red and yellow
flashes from frame to frame,
giant fist clenched,
ready
to SMACK the masked bandit in the final frame!

I place a sheet of paper next to that frame,
select a pencil
and spread an array of crayons,
ready
to draw and color
my own Captain Marvel,
giant fist delivering the mighty SMACK!

I sketch the fist at the end of Captain Marvel's
extended arm
as it decks the bandit,
his gun and bank bag flying
from his hands,
then draw
the balloon containing the mighty SMACK!

I lean back from the table, smile at my
accomplishment,
prepare to add color: red, yellow, flesh
for the fist, but as I apply,
I notice the colors in the comic book
do not match mine,
those seem and feel grainy, mine waxy smooth.

My artist mind wonders why, so I borrow
my grandmother's
magnifying glass, the one that helps her read,
and place it over the comic fist.
The fist is made of dots, hundreds and hundreds

of little dots, all the colors are dots,
and I begin to wonder just how that can be.

I decide to ask my art teacher about the dots—she
says I can do that, too, but I have to use
sharp colored pencils instead of crayons, then
adds, "Let's learn," and goes
to the cabinet, takes a box of colored pencils
and sets me to sharpening them.
She takes a large book of famous artists from
another cabinet, and as she opens it, says,
"I know the artist who made the dots famous."

She turns the pages until she finds a painting
that covers two pages and says,
"His name is Seurat, and this is his painting. If you
look closely, you will see it is made up of
hundreds and hundreds of dots, just like the comic
book." The painting has grainy trees, grainy bushes,
grainy people, grainy dogs, and a grainy monkey.
Everything in the painting is grainy,
made up of thousands and thousands of dots.

"The style is called pointilisma," she says, "and
the name of the painting is
'A Sunday Afternoon on the Island of the Grand Jatte.'"
"He's French," she adds, and brings her
magnifying glass so I can get a closer look at
the dots. "He made the dots with the stiff
bristles of his brush. Printers learned how to do
it with machines,
and that's why Captain Marvel is made of dots."

I take out my partly colored drawing and start
to place flesh dots on the fist and black dots
on the SMASH!
After an hour of placing dot next to dot,
my fingers, closing to an aching fist,
are glad
printers learned how to do it with machines.
So that's how I learned
about the dots made famous by Georges Seurat.

winter

rose rims thin along the length
of the horizon
just below the grey threat of snow
looming full-bellied,
is that a flake?—
uneasy, I am driving towards it

crows in winter

along the Rio del Yeso
black preying
leaves
in a tree
unlike leaves change trees

when the sun almost died in December
about the Aztec god Nanahuatzin

the ugly skinned god
deformed
in body and face

despised
by all the Aztec
gods

fed the sun, became
the sun,
savior of gods and man

kept the earth from
becoming
dark

kept the earth from
becoming
cold

when he leapt into
the faltering
fire

dim at the southern
rim
of the morning horizon

where god and man
thought
the sun would die

not have the strength
to return
north along the rim—

he leapt in
silence
except for the crackle

of his ugly
skin—
then warmth as the sun

moved north
along
the rim and god and man

cheered
and cheered
and cheered and cheered

our savior sun, Nanahuatzin

Christmas Eve

Kneel before the manger scene,
meditate
among the calm flicker of votive flames,
adore
the child lying there

but do not think
of
the prophecy of a man torn
on the cross
by nail, thorn, lash, and spear,

and do not think
of
the twice bitten apple,
of
the first murdered brother,
of
the destruction of two cities,

and do not think
of
the slaughter of first born,
of
the walls tumbling at Jericho,

and do not think
of
crusaders putting heathens to the sword,
of
holy inquisitors,
of
witches burned and hanged at Salem,

and do not think
of
concentration gas and nuclear explosion,
of
planes crashing into towers,
of
suicide
explosion, explosion, explosion

in the very place where the apple
was eaten,
where a brother again kills brother,
where
a city in factions destroys itself,

oh do not think
of
any of this, simply Kneel before the
manger scene,
meditate
among the flicker of votive flames,
adore
the child lying there

An Artist Observes Two Winter Scenes

I'm amazed at how that tree
takes up space
in
oh
just such a natural way,
takes
its pose, limbs outstretched
up, out

blue sky showing through

and

I'm amazed at how that man
sits
in the coffee shop
in
oh
just such a natural way,
takes
his pose, limbs bent
so hands
can
grasp the cup
and
hold it steaming to his lips,

outlined
as the sun shines

through the plate glass window

the incurable academic discusses
a snowflake

it tumbled through cloud this wonder
of nature onto my sweater sleeve
like absolutely no other ever I understand

six delicate branches in my magnifying glass
begun as a speck of dust becoming
the nucleus of a droplet of water cooling around it

high up in cloud becoming ice, attracting
molecule upon molecule, growing branches,
side branches, ridges, ribs, rims, rime,

but here I go again becoming the academic
instead of just enjoying the crystal beauty
unlike no other ever upon my sleeve
yet there is something of beauty in how it
becomes, for this complex beauty is simple
physics, chemistry, geometry—

now for the process of melting. . . . .

Reference—Ken Libbrecht's Field Guide to Snowflakes.